Our Very Smart, Violent Children

William G. Hegarty
Chief of Police, ret.

With Steven W. Dieleman

© Copyright 2001 Kent Intermediate School District
2930 Knapp, N.E., Grand Rapids, Michigan 49525

Designed by Jim VanHill
JVH Graphics Group Inc.

Library of Congress Control Number: 2001087357

William G. Hegarty, Chief of Police, ret.
With Steven W. Dieleman
Our Very Smart, Violent Children

First Edition
Second Printing

ISBN 0-9708553-0-3 (pbk.)

For more information, contact the

Kent Intermediate School District
2930 Knapp, NE
Grand Rapids, Michigan 49525
(616) 364-1333
E-mail: sdielem@remc8.k12.mi.us

Foreword

It was the beginning of another day at the high school. The students were in the hallways, gathered around their lockers, or in the large cafeteria, enjoying their friendships or quietly preparing for the day. The mood was good – friendly and peaceful. After all, it was a "good" school – academically and socially.

Until the awful sound of gunfire erupted.

At first, some believed it was simply fireworks being playfully discharged. But these thoughts were quickly erased by the dreadful sights and sounds of students screaming, running, and falling to the floor, covered with blood from wounds to their heads and young bodies.

Some were dead, and others were seriously

injured and desperately crying for help. And the gunfire persisted, striking more students and some of the teachers.

Near the middle of the hysterical crowd, another student stood – with a gun in his hand. Without speaking, he calmly aimed and fired his weapon, frequently reloading and deliberately firing again. And again.

Everyone knew him. He was a very "smart" student, possessed a high grade point average, and loved computers. He appeared alone a lot but was never in trouble at school.

And there he was – trying to kill everyone.

Why was he doing this?

And what are the reasons for these kinds of violent acts in our schools? Are there programs designed to prevent them, and do they really work? Are there procedures for intercepting a threat or a plan to kill people in schools? Is there a practical procedure for schools about how to respond to violent incidents, and is it designed to protect students and employees?

And, most importantly, how can our schools and

communities come together and more constructively help our children grow – to develop all of their emotional, social, and moral abilities – the most essential ingredients of their personalities?

These are a few of the very important questions communities are desperately trying to answer.

And that is the intent of this short, practical book – to briefly answer these questions and to outline a "model plan" – a blueprint for any community that intends to respond to the needs of their children, their families, and schools.

At this point, I must admit that I am not a psychologist or a social worker, and I was never a school principal or a teacher. Worst of all, some people hurtfully say that I do not write "very well" – too simple, very direct, and, at times, unusually blunt.

But there is a reason for these "deficiencies."

For more than twenty-five (25) years, I was a police chief.

Altogether, I enjoyed thirty-three (33) years of law enforcement in California, New York, and Michigan. It was a career that permitted me to achieve all of my professional goals by serving people and helping them live more safely; I absolutely loved it. Most of the time.

Yes, there were some very difficult moments – incidents reported to the police, for example, that touched my personal feelings, i.e., the death or serious injury of children, etc. I can still feel the "sting" of a telephone call at three o'clock in the morning about the fatal shooting of a young boy on a street corner in one of our neighborhoods.

And, unfortunately, this kind of very disturbing call was becoming increasingly common. The incidents prompted us to urgently find answers – answers about the identity of the suspects, the causes or reasons for the shootings, and programs that we could adopt to prevent the loss of more young lives.

Our search for answers went far beyond the traditional role of "policing."

With the help of many people in the community, we began to achieve these goals. After spending many years together in the neighborhoods, all of us eventually felt a very strong sense of relief and accomplishment; the "partnership of commitment" to protect lives and property worked.

Fewer lives were tragically lost, serious injuries from gunshot wounds decreased, and people enjoyed a higher quality of life for their children and families.

It was a very gratifying feeling.

I eventually left "police chiefing" and began to work with our schools; I believed I could uniquely help our communities by blending the lessons of a very unusual career with my knowledge about our children and schools.

But, shortly afterwards, the shootings began again – and this time they were occurring in our schools; many young students, randomly shot by other students, were tragically killed or seriously injured.

And I felt the "sting" again – the need and the responsibility to do something or, at the very least, find a few answers about the reasons for these deadly incidents and attempt to prevent them.

Remindful of my earlier years in law enforcement, I initially tried to more completely understand the incidents, i.e., the personal history of the suspects, the reasons for the shootings, the circumstances of the incidents, police responses, etc. After doing a lot of research, I became increasingly frustrated – frustrated because I could not find a match between the apparent causes of the shootings that I identified and the eventual commentaries of many "authorities" after the incidents – commentaries about how to prevent or respond to them. For the most part, their "answers" were political, emotional, or legal statements that were expressed according to personal agendas; they were unrelated to the identified causes of the incidents or the pattern that was becoming very evident.

Political leaders were, for example, distributing countless news releases, holding news conferences, or appearing on nightly news broadcasts with all of the "experts," talking superficially about the need for more federal and state statutes regarding handgun control and the affects of video games, television programming, etc.

Unfortunately, I strongly believe that all of this "talk" or effort to legislatively prevent or control the problem will do little or nothing to prevent the young man from entering a school facility and discharging or detonating weapons in a crowded cafeteria, auditorium, or library.

We must begin to correctly identify the causes of the problem and respond to them in a more meaningful and unified way.

And that is the intent of this message.

The book consists of four (4) parts: it begins in Chapter One (1) with a general Viewpoint about the Causes of Violent Incidents in our Schools. This assessment is critical if we intend to more responsively prevent these tragedies in the future.

Chapter Two (2) is a Model Plan for Schools and Communities; it consists of programs designed to prevent violent activity and to help our children develop all of their "intelligences" – their emotional, social, moral, and intellectual abilities.

Chapter Three (3) is about Preparatory Steps or Programs to Intercept Potential Violent Incidents in Schools. Designed for school administrators and employees, it outlines several practical steps to adopt that may help schools intercept or prevent a tragedy.

Chapter Four (4) outlines the need for schools and communities to adopt a procedure about How to Respond To Violent Incidents in Schools. Accordingly, a Model Procedure for Schools is outlined in the Appendix; it is a very complete blueprint of outlined responsibilities for all school employees about responding to critical incidents. And it also provides school employees and students with a very important resource regarding their personal safety.

Appropriately, the Conclusion of the book is a general outline of The Process of Developing Community and Financial Support for Programs that are recommended for schools and communities.

And that is the chronological format of this message: a viewpoint about the causes of violent incidents in our schools, programs designed to prevent them, preparatory steps to intercept them, and a practical procedure for schools about how to safely respond to them.

It is relatively short, concisely outlined, and practical.

It is also a very strong message about the

development of our children – and the responsibilities of parents, schools, and communities.

And because of this holistic approach, the book is also very unique.

After many years in law enforcement, I sincerely hope that "Our Very Smart, Violent Children" becomes our "shared vision" – our "Model Plan" to help our children grow and live more safely.

It is the only way to prevent "the awful sound of gunfire" and to respond to the needs of young personalities in a more meaningful, unified way.

Our Very Smart, Violent Children

More About the Author

Prior to his retirement in 1998, William G. Hegarty was the Chief of Police of the City of Grand Rapids, Michigan, for sixteen (16) years.

Before his appointment to this position in 1981, he served in police departments in California, New York, and Michigan.

During his police management career, he received many national, state, and local awards for his accomplishments. He was, for example, the recipient of the highest international award for "Quality in Law Enforcement" in 1996 and received the highest award in the State of Michigan for "Community Service" in 1995 from the Michigan Bar Association.

He received Bachelor of Science and Master of

Science degrees from Michigan State University and eventually became an Assistant Professor at this university. He is also a graduate of the National Executive Institute of the Federal Bureau of Investigation.

After thirty-three (33) years in law enforcement, he is a Life Member of the International Association of Chiefs of Police and the Michigan Association of Chiefs of Police.

At the present time, he is a consultant to the Kent Intermediate School District, presenting training programs and workshops regarding "How to Prevent and Respond to Violent Incidents in Schools." He also provides consulting services for schools regarding general school security issues.

Acknowledgements

I sincerely thank Dr. George Woons, the Superintendent of the Kent Intermediate School District in Grand Rapids, Michigan, and the Associate Superintendents, Michael S. Weiler and Gerald L. Hunsburger, for their support and leadership.

I am also very thankful to the Kent Intermediate School District Board: Dan E. Biddick, Reverend Ralph Carey, Andrea Haidle, Carol A. Perry, and Fred Thorne.

The source of encouragement and assistance for this effort was Steven W. Dieleman, a consultant to the Kent Intermediate School District; he was, and is, extremely helpful and, again, I am grateful.

And to Marie Neil, the Director of the General Education Services Department, David Buell, the

Assistant Director and Ron Koehler, the Director of Communications Services at the Kent Intermediate School District, thank you for your guidance and support.

John K. Belaski and Cheryl Blair are also consultants to the Kent Intermediate School District, and I thank them for their continuing help and commitment to "youth development." And I thank Gretchen VandenBerg, Polly Ranschaert, and Jacquelyn Bush for their very patient help during the preparation of our work.

One final note: I am very grateful to all of the school superintendents, principals, assistant principals, teachers, and other school employees that I met and worked with during my "careers"; I possess complete respect for their efforts and commitment to our children. And I sincerely thank them. All of us do.

Contents

The Causes of Violent Incidents in Schools: A Viewpoint

Chapter 1

Our Very Smart, Violent Children

The Causes of Violent Incidents in Schools: A Viewpoint

It is very clear that the foremost goal of our schools is the intellectual growth of our children; the process of developing verbal and numerical skills is, for example, a vital part of building very young personalities and providing them with the technical "tools of life."

And there are many measurements of this process; multiple tests and assessments are administered, standards are promulgated, corresponding curriculums are designed with the intent of achieving uniformity of subject material, and eventual judgments are rendered about the technical competency of students and the quality of schools.

And the results of these efforts are becoming

very apparent; in many communities, our children are becoming more academically "smart."

But something is very wrong or at least critically absent from this process; and, regretfully, the problem is growing.

It is about our failure to develop all of the other "intelligences" – the emotional, social, and moral abilities of our children, or those psychological tools of life that are the most essential ingredients of our personalities.

If there was, for example, a standardized test that assessed the emotional "intelligence" or growth of students, the scores could be alarmingly low. And, directly after the results were publicly released, there would be countless community meetings and political statements about the emotional development of students, the abilities of teachers, and the quality of our schools.

But, during this "rush to judgment," it should be remembered that it is our attitudes about the development of our children that may be the most important cause of this serious problem – and it is not, for the most part, the fault of our teachers or schools. After all, we emphatically tell them that the intellectual growth of students, increasingly measured in standardized tests, is their most important responsibility.

Unfortunately, we are the most blameworthy – and the reasons are relatively clear. Very disturbingly, it appears that we *wrongfully* believe that the responsibility of "educating" or developing our children:

1. is solely a matter of developing their technical tools of life, the intellectual abilities of becoming academically smart, i.e., test scores, grade point averages, etc.;

2. is not about the growth of the other intelligences – their emotional, social, and moral skills, and that emotional skills, for example, do not affect intellectual abilities or their growth;

3. solely belongs to the teachers in our schools;

4. is exclusively about the technical competency of students during these critical developmental years; and

5. does not, for the most part, belong to the parents or the "learning environments" away from the school facility that affect the development of young personalities.

It is these kinds of *wrongful* beliefs – about the development of our children, the role of our schools, and the responsibilities of parents that are largely contributing to this critical problem in many communities.

Historically, the role of the parent was extremely important during this developmental process; the homes of our children became the most important "emotional classrooms" and the educators, i.e., parents, completely accepted their responsibility for the psychological growth of their children. But these "schools" are increasingly closing. For many very young men and women, the contemporary home is simply becoming a source of food, shelter, and financial support. In many cases, it is not a classroom of emotional growth and it is not a caring and respectful environment that breeds feelings of acceptance, personal worth, and moral growth. It does not equip children with the ability to independently reason and render ethical judgments. It does not permit children to display and understand personal feelings and constructively manage them and, very importantly, it does not teach them about accepting personal responsibility and being accountable for their own conduct; after all, many parental "teachers" rarely do it.

And this flawed learning environment begins at a very early age. Many parents, for example, allege that time restrictions, occupational goals and responsibilities, social commitments, and other related reasons do not permit them to tend to the psychological needs of their children. Others feel that they do not even possess the abilities for teaching or assisting the development of verbal and numerical skills. And there are parents who leave the process of developing social and moral abilities to their own emotional displays that are, at times, more harmful than helpful to their children. And, finally, there are parents who functionally become "the children of their children," subordinating their parental responsibilities to their own emotional needs of becoming "accepted" or "approved" by their own children.

Increasingly, the home is not, for many young children, a secure, caring environment; the feelings of comfort or loving acceptance by a parent do not exist. The healthy development of emotional and moral abilities, for example, is either absent or becomes distorted; and for the child, "anger management" may simply mean to harmfully display it without any sense of personal accountability because of absent parental authority.

Eventually, children go to the social environment of their schools and their friends and acquaintances to "become somebody," to become emotionally fed and learn more about the psychological tools of life.

They begin to search for their "other family," another source of being accepted, finding personal worth and displaying feelings that are shared and supported without being rejected or abandoned.

And the search becomes depressingly painful. As they become older, they quickly learn that the social environment of schools is very stratified, that there are silent rules regarding their "acceptability" and that, in many instances, their abilities or beliefs about themselves do not match the standards of belonging to the right "family," social group, etc. If they are not, for example, athletically or academically "qualified," are not a member of student government, or are too short, too fat, too "dorky" or, worst of all, not "cool," they become disqualified and rejected and begin to desperately feel unwanted, unaccepted, or rejected again.

And, at this point, feelings of anger instead of feelings of comfort begin to more completely fill the young mind. The psychological tools of life have become increasingly distorted. The emotional intelligence becomes either regressively retarded or skewed by hostility, and the social abilities or eventual moral judgments of the young men or women become flawed.

But the search goes on for the right "other family" – other students or acquaintances who share their feelings. Their need to become somebody, somebody important, becomes obsessively stressed and eventually distorts their other intelligences.

And they eventually find it: other students,

usually "outcasts" from the stratified social environment of the school with the same feelings and needs — technically smart, depressed, or emotionally starving and with varied levels of anger and hostility. And they come together in every way — intellectually and emotionally and in the more common, conforming aspects of dress, language, and personal interests. The bonding grows; it grows because one of the essential elements of their mutual identity is to hatefully identify a common enemy. Those persons, groups, or activities that, in the past, rejected them, ignored them, or in some way displayed disrespectful, hurtful feelings, are the targets of their wrath.

And the more hateful the "family" becomes, the stronger they feel about belonging to the "right" group and about their own worth. Feeling the comfort of and finally being accepted by another "school of emotional growth" that will become their source of the "real" psychological tools of life is the achievement of a very important emotional goal for them.

But these are only a few of the reasons for the growth of gangs, "Trench Coat Mafias," or other deviant "families" that are increasingly doing the traditional work of schools, parents, and, yes, churches. Increasingly, the "outsiders" are going to these sources to find personal comfort and identity. But the other tragedy of this trend is that a common psychological denominator of these groups is legitimized anger: feeling and displaying hostility without guilt. If these dangerous attitudes are combined with the intellectual skills that are being very efficiently developed by our schools, very smart yet disturbed children, loyally supporting each other and feeling very confident about themselves, may collectively plan and commit violent activities. Most certainly, these displays permit them to vent their mutual hostility without guilt and reach a level of "power" that, heretofore, did not exist in their lives and is not achievable in any other legal or moral manner.

In an April 9-12, 2000, *New York Times* series of articles entitled "Rampage Killers," it was reported that many young men committing deadly shootings at school facilities sought and obtained reinforcement from their peers and boasted of their plans. The *Times* additionally reported that their study of one hundred (100) incidents during the past fifty (50) years revealed many other insightful findings. For example, most of the school assailants:

1. ". . . left a road map of red flags, spending months plotting their attacks and accumulating weapons, talking openly of their plans . . . ." and ". . . give lots of warning and even tell people explicitly what they plan to do.";

2. displayed blatant signs of serious mental health problems; family members, friends, mental health professionals, teachers, and the police either missed or dismissed the aforementioned signs or independently possessed knowledge about mental health problems and did not communicate with one another or attempt to collectively intervene;

3. carried semi-automatic weapons that were easily obtained and, in many cases, legally purchased. It should be noted that local police departments, in most states, cannot

legally access the mental health records of persons intending to purchase and lawfully possess handguns;

4. were not habitual offenders or convicted of serious violent offenses;

5. were not under the influence of alcohol or illegal drugs at the time of the attack;

6. did not, according to many noted authorities in the fields of forensic psychiatry or psychology, act "impulsively," "randomly," "suddenly," or "senselessly," i.e., the shootings were committed after "months" of prior planning; and

7. did not commit the attacks because of video games, movies, television programming, or musical lyrics although, in several cases, such entertainment sources, with peer support, may have "detonated" the mental disorder and "precipitated" the violent attack.

Unfortunately, and potentially tragically, this "profile" exists in all of our schools and communities:

very smart, disturbed young men and women, possessing the psychological ingredients and abilities to commit violent activities without emotional attachments, fear of accountability or guilt – waiting for the detonating or precipitating event that will emotionally catapult them to a level of acceptability or power that never existed before in their lives.

And ". . . talking openly of their plans . . . ." telling people ". . . explicitly what they plan to do."

We cannot distance ourselves from this problem anymore; it is not "their problem" in another city or neighborhood, and the suspects are not "those people," a stereotypical term that creates instant personal comfort by believing that the problem is geographically distant or personally unrelated. The suspects are not young men from poor, minority neighborhoods in larger cities, habitual criminals, or drug addicts; they are not academically inferior or necessarily from the homes of single, unemployed, and unskilled parents.

Again, the "profile" of the very "smart," violent personality exists in all of our school districts and communities.

And, after the next shooting occurs in a school, our school boards and administrators will receive countless telephone calls and letters from parents about school security and the safety of their children. Because of their fears, hundreds of parents will attend more community meetings and, in part, ask the questions "Why did they do it?" and "How can we prevent it in our school?"

Simultaneously, political leaders will begin to distribute more news releases, hold more news conferences, and appear on nightly news broadcasts with all of the "experts," talking about more federal and state statutes regarding handgun control and the affects of video games.

They simply do not get it.

All of the security technology and efforts to legislatively prevent or control this problem will do little or nothing to prevent the young man with the relatively high grade point average and disturbed personality from entering a school facility and discharging or detonating weapons in a crowded cafeteria, auditorium, or library.

We must begin to correctly identify the cause of the problem and respond to it in a more meaningful and unified way.

And that is the intent of this book.

It is frequently stated that a community possesses the responsibility of collectively developing the total personality of our children, i.e., "It takes a village . . . ." But, unfortunately, this belief exists without the support of reality; there is not, in most communities, a coordinated effort to achieve this goal or even to correctly identify the apparent causes of the problem.

With the leadership of our elected officials and our school districts, communities must come together and collectively say that the responsibility of educating our children:

1. is about developing their whole personality, all of their emotional, social, moral, and intellectual abilities;

2. is not simply a matter of developing their technical skills in the classroom or insisting that the only measurement of achievement

is a high grade point average or becoming academically "qualified";

3. belongs to the entire community because the process of learning and the development of our youth is constant; it extends beyond the classrooms of our schools and is dependent on the other very important "teachers" – parents, families, peers, clergy, etc. – those who significantly affect the psychological growth of our children;

4. means that we must adopt programs in our school curriculums designed to achieve the aforementioned goals and expand the role of school facilities to support our mutual efforts in the communities; and

5. is about extending our educational efforts to the homes and communities of our students with the belief that we must constructively affect the environment that emotionally, socially, and morally "molds" them and builds their psychological tools of life.

If we intend to prevent the loss of more young lives in our schools and help develop "very smart, healthy children," we must strongly adopt this community or "shared vision" and begin to initiate or expand programs designed to achieve the outlined goals.

Programs Designed to Prevent Violent Incidents in Schools:
A Model Plan for Schools and Communities

Chapter 2

Our Very Smart, Violent Children

Introductory Comments

Because of the scope of the problem that is described in the first Chapter of this book and our need to specifically respond to the outlined causes of young, violent activity, it is necessary to design or recommend programs that are more holistic – programs that affect all of the developmental stages of our children, from early childhood to the final years of high school.

Most certainly, it is about adopting programs that are intended to specifically develop the whole personality of our children, all of their "intelligences."

And it is about constructively affecting their personal environments, outside the classroom, that frequently are the sources of their "learning disabilities" or emotional difficulties.

That is the only valid way to achieve our foremost goal: to prevent violent activity in our schools and communities.

There is a growing number of "program evaluation" studies that clearly tell us another very important message: if schools and communities come together and jointly accept the responsibility of adopting the outlined programs, the results of their efforts may cause other very important results for our children and families:

1. higher levels of achievement;

2. fewer incidents of reported assaults, general criminal activity, or delinquency;

3. less truancy;

4. lower levels of drug and alcohol abuse;

5. fewer violations of "rules of conduct" and disciplinary proceedings in our schools;

6. more parental participation in school activities and parental support programs; and

7. a stronger partnership between schools and communities.

The programs that are briefly outlined in the

Model Plan for Schools and Communities Chapter are not inclusive, but they are, from the experiences and viewpoint of this author, the most important and validated efforts to achieve the outlined goals.

And, finally, the format of the Model Plan was designed to provide schools and communities with a general blueprint or "menu" of programs that may be briefly reviewed and adopted according to individual needs or circumstances. Because of the purpose and outline of this book, it was not intended to be a complete compilation of resource material about programs or their applicability in all of our schools or communities.

Early Childhood Learning Program

Brief Summary

It has been frequently stated that the most critical learning period in the lives of our children generally occurs during the first five (5) years of development. And it is during this time that very young personalities are being formed – the ability to intellectually learn and reason is being developed and the "emotional intelligence" is being created.

Unfortunately, and because of the reasons that were outlined in the first Chapter of this book, this vital learning process is frequently yielding results or "psychological products" that are intellectually or emotionally damaged or, at least, functionally needful.

Increasingly, many very young children are

living in homes or environments that are psychologically and physically debilitating; in both affluent and poor households, for example, parental abandonment or neglect is not uncommon. And, in many circumstances, there are family histories of illiteracy, alcohol, drug, or criminal activity, unattended physical and emotional injuries, poor dietary habits, and unsanitary conditions without proper medical or dental care.

And, in the midst of these environments, many very young personalities are being "molded" and developed with a strong belief of being personally worthless and unwanted. In other words, the most critical learning period is increasingly creating young minds that are programmed to fail – academically, emotionally, and socially.

If we expect our students to eventually excel, intellectually and emotionally, we must develop and adopt a radically different approach to this growing problem – an approach that causes the proper development of these young personalities during this critical age period.

Most certainly, we must develop the abilities to

properly learn before we can expect our children to actually learn after they enroll in kindergarten or a formal school program. And we must develop these abilities in a safe, caring environment that is designed to respond to all of their needs – intellectual, emotional, medical, nutritional, etc.

It is strongly recommended, therefore, that Early Childhood Learning Centers be created by our schools and communities. Very briefly, the Centers would:

1. provide an affordable, holistic learning environment for children between the ages of three (3) and five (5);

2. strongly encourage the development of the verbal and numerical skills of children and their general intellectual abilities to learn;

3. help children grow emotionally, socially, and morally by learning to identify, understand, and manage their feelings, together with other related behaviors that may assist their psychological or personal development;

4. identify and respond to any medical, dental, or nutritional need of the children;

5. work with the parents and families of children at the Center with the intent of developing their parenting skills or other tools that would help them create a more helpful learning environment at home; and

6. periodically assess the intellectual, physical, and psychological development of children at the Center for the purpose of identifying and "remedializing" any need or weakness.

Furthermore, the Centers would be staffed by school employees, community service providers, students or interns from local universities and colleges specializing in elementary education or early child development, senior volunteers, and volunteer parents. In very general terms, the school employees and community service providers would accept responsibilities related to Center management and program coordination. The students would be assigned to the supervised responsibilities of "learning facilitators," and the volunteers would perform a variety of support duties for the Center and the staff.

It is additionally recommended that financial

support for the Centers become, at least initially, a shared responsibility; a formula may be designed, for example, that equitably builds a partnership between the schools, the local governmental unit, employers of the participating parents, and the parents of attending children.

Our Very Smart, Violent Children

Learning Support Teams Program

Brief Summary

In the Brief Summary of the Early Childhood Learning Program, it was emphasized that ". . . many very young children are living in homes and environments that are psychologically and physically debilitating . . . ."

A very dedicated teacher recently asked a pointed question about her role in the general learning process of the children in her class:

"How can I teach a child to learn, for a few hours a day, if he spends the rest of his time in an environment that is emotionally killing him?"

She eventually answered her own question:

"I have to go out . . . to the homes and

neighborhoods of my children . . . during the evenings and weekends and at least try to work with their parents or family members . . . help them with their problems . . . and maybe my students will eventually come to school less emotionally damaged and more interested in learning."

It is unreasonable to expect our teachers, especially in elementary school grades, to reach higher levels of student achievement if they do not possess the resources to affect the environments that are psychologically damaging the intellectual skills of their students; if a child is being emotionally "battered" in the home, we cannot expect him or her to academically excel during the very brief school day. And, until schools possess at least the ability to respond to these conditions, the very intelligent, emotionally damaged child will not reach higher levels of intellectual development.

It is strongly recommended, therefore, that Learning Support Teams be created and assigned to elementary schools. The Teams would, for example:

1.   be assigned to and support teachers during

their efforts to assist students who display lower achievement levels or general behavior problems;

2. provide extensive tutorial or remedial assistance to selected students;

3. attempt to work with families of selected students for the purpose of creating more interest in and support for the educational process of the assigned children;

4. develop strong relationships with the school support staff – counselors, social workers, etc. – and other community and mental health services for the purpose of referring identified family or personal problems to the proper authority for treatment or disposition; and

5. periodically meet with assigned teachers, other school staff members, and community and mental health services to review assigned cases and to collaboratively outline educational and behavioral goals, together with more detailed "action plans," for the assigned student.

Mentoring and Tutoring Programs

Brief Summary

Mentoring and Tutoring Programs for students need to be adopted or expanded in our schools and communities. According to the results of many research studies, our children are increasingly searching for a role model, someone who will become a vital part of their lives during their critical childhood and adolescent years.

And mentoring programs *work*; higher grades, less absenteeism, fewer rule violations, decreased levels of drug and alcohol use, and higher college and university enrollments are a few of the empirical results of studies during the past five (5) years.

If mentoring programs are designed and

adopted in schools with the intent of supporting the goals of this Model Plan, or the outlined recommended programs, they would unquestionably assist students and directly respond to the many problems affecting our contemporary children.

There are three (3) general kinds of mentoring and tutoring programs: personal development, career, and academic. These programs are excellent approaches to "youth development" and should be jointly adopted in the school environment with the support of the community.

More specifically, it is recommended that peer mentoring and tutoring programs be adopted; peer mentoring responds to the personal needs of the mentored student and positively affects the social environment of a school. For example, students in the upper grade levels becoming the mentors or tutors of students in lower grades will encourage:

1. the growth of the intellectual or academic skills of the mentored or tutored student;

2. the development of a personal relationship that will psychologically assist the mentored

student;

3. feelings of being accepted and becoming a respected "friend" in the socially stratified environment of the school by the mentored student;

4. the development of leadership skills by the mentoring or tutoring student; and

5. the belief among all students that the needs, not the differences, of other students are very important and that all students collectively possess the responsibility of "helping a friend."

Because of the growing effects or behavioral influences of contemporary peers, these kinds of programs are, especially in the school environment, very important among all of the efforts to help students and the general educational process.

Curriculum Program

Brief Summary

The most appropriate way of introducing the purpose of this recommendation is a recent quotation from another elementary school teacher:

"We can spend months and years helping our kids to become "smart," but their test scores and grades may not show it until someone does something about their emotional lives, their feelings and attitudes – they are the "killers" and it all seems to come from their homes, the environment away from the classroom . . . it is destroying a lot of our work and is academically injuring them."

Again, we cannot expect our children to become academically "smart" if their abilities to learn are damaged or distorted by their emotional lives or psychological needs.

And that is the foremost reason for holistically recommending many programs in this Chapter; our children must grow emotionally, socially, and morally during the development of their intellectual abilities.

It is strongly recommended, therefore, that schools adopt "learning modules" in their curriculums that are designed to provide students with "life skills" that will help them psychologically grow and develop all of their personal abilities during their educational experiences.

A practical program, for example, that actually simulates "life experiences" will encourage students to learn a variety of skills in a more meaningful manner. Contrary to the traditional classroom setting, these kinds of programs may consist of practical exercises that realistically portray employment and social environments, interpersonal or family relationships, and ethical problems that may commonly exist for young personalities.

Simulating these kinds of experiences and

educationally assigning students to varied roles and responsibilities will present many vital and exciting learning opportunities. For example, the program will encourage students to:

1. develop their abilities to independently reason and render ethical judgments;

2. display and understand personal feelings and constructively manage them;

3. feel more confident about being accepted and about their own personal worth and growth;

4. accept personal responsibility and learn more about being accountable for their own conduct; and

5. enjoy the process of learning and setting personal goals that may cause higher levels of intellectual and personal achievement.

Accordingly, there are several validated curriculums that are strongly recommended:

Character Education – programs designed to teach and support fundamental moral and ethical skills, i.e., accepting responsibility and accountability, respect for others, etc.

Health Education – programs designed to help children understand and manage their physical and emotional abilities.

Academic Service Learning – programs designed to help children reach higher levels of achievement in the language arts, social studies, and math and sciences by developing their "practical application" skills in school or community environments.

Life Management Skills – programs designed to teach personal life management skills, i.e., setting personal goals, developing analytical abilities, "decision making," etc.

Conflict Management – programs designed to teach conflict mediation and resolution skills.

Family Resource Centers Program

Brief Summary

It was stated in the first Chapter of this book, "We must adopt a 'community vision' and begin to initiate or expand programs designed to achieve the outlined goals."

" . . . communities must come together and collectively say that the responsibility of educating our children:

> 3. "belongs to the entire community because the process of learning and the development of our youth is constant, extending beyond the classrooms of our schools and is dependent on other very important 'teachers,' i.e., parents, families,

peers, clergy, etc.; and

4. "we must adopt programs . . . and expand the role of school facilities to support our mutual efforts . . . ."

To accomplish these very important responsibilities, it is strongly recommended that school facilities become "centers" for students, families, and communities after the normal school day is complete, i.e., late afternoons and evenings. A collaborative planning effort of school, local government, law enforcement, and community service organizations should identify, with the help of interested students and parents, the foremost needs or problems affecting their children and families and collectively design or adopt programs that will correctively respond to them.

And the school facility would become the centralized focal point of this work, the "centers" of all of these combined efforts. For example, students could participate in tutorial programs, mentoring activities, varied intramural activities, special interest clubs (i.e., computers, foreign languages, etc.), counseling services, community service, recreational and social activities, career and college orientation activities, etc.

Additionally, the school facility would become a family or community "center." Programs and activities that are related to youth and family development, parental responsibilities, parent-teacher activities and meetings, family recreational programs, community service activities, and general community meetings are a few of the events that will help our children, build strong families, and become vital community activities.

The financial support of the "centers" should also become a shared responsibility because the results of the proposed programs could, or will, positively affect all aspects of the community resulting in higher levels of student achievement, fewer incidents of reported delinquency or criminal activity (especially after school hours, i.e., 3:00 – 6:00 p.m.), more parental support programs and activities, and a stronger partnership between schools and communities.

Our Very Smart, Violent Children

Student Counseling Programs

Brief Summary

Student counseling programs or services should be created or expanded in all of our schools. It is vitally necessary to provide a safe, trustful program for students if they wish to confidentially receive help about a personal or emotional problem.

Additionally, programs about anger management or control, conflict mediation or resolution, etc., are essential and a very important part of any effort to develop "life skills" for students and support the recommended curriculum learning modules.

"No Stranger in Our School" Program

Brief Summary

Schools should individually and personally assign students to members of the school staff. The intent of this program is to permit every student to develop a personal relationship with an "advisor" and feel that he or she is not a "stranger" in the school. The growth of these friendships will, for the most part, help students grow academically and at least feel more emotionally attached to his or her "friend" and the school community. More specifically, the school staff, meeting weekly with individually assigned students, may assist them with academic assignments, relationships with family or peers, or any other matter that is needfully expressed by the students.

Another vital product of this program is that the school staff will eventually be able to not only help the student and family in a more personalized manner, but also become more aware of potential student problems that may be referred to school administrators for review and disposition.

School Disciplinary Procedures – Rules of Conduct

Brief Summary

School disciplinary procedures and "rules of conduct" are absolutely imperative and must be fairly and consistently enforced. These practices may become more effective if they are formulated and conducted with the advisement of other community resources such as law enforcement, family court, mental health services, etc.

Student Responsibility Centers are one promising model for improving traditional school disciplinary procedures. This program helps students accept responsibility for their actions and modify their behavior. In this model, teachers are empowered to remove disruptive students from their classrooms;

these students would report directly to a Student Responsibility Center. With the assistance of assigned school staff, students must develop plans to address their problems and improve their behavior before returning to the assigned classroom. The student and the teacher must mutually agree on the student's plan of action. This model of student accountability is implemented in selected school districts throughout the country and is intended to more correctively replace the traditional punitive model for minor violations of school rules.

Mandatory Psychological Assessment – Suspended and Expelled Students

Brief Summary

There are, according to many sources, students in our schools who possess some form of mental disorder or serious emotional difficulty.

In many of these cases, parents arrange treatment programs – counseling services, pharmaceutical treatment, etc. – for their children that are privately and confidentially administered and designed to either correct or control the identified problem.

For other students, a mental health or emotional problem may, unfortunately, exist without being diagnostically identified or treated. Most of the time, these students satisfactorily complete the formal educational process. But there are afflicted students who may display – chronically or acutely – attitudes or behaviors that are harmful to themselves or others. And, after the violations are reported, they are eventually suspended or expelled from the school by the proper authority.

It is strongly recommended that if any student displays the aforementioned conduct and is suspended or expelled from school, he or she will not be permitted to return to the school or any school facility until a psychologist or psychiatrist, specializing in childhood or adolescent behavior and retained by the school district of the requested reinstatement or enrollment, "certifies" that the student is not harmful to himself or others.

Very simply, this recommendation is intended to protect the school community – physically, emotionally, and legally – and to help the suspended or expelled student.

To facilitate the recommendations, school districts may wish to jointly retain the services of a specialized psychologist or psychiatrist and review the feasibility of creating and sharing a centralized information system that at least outlines the most serious student disciplinary records – suspensions, expulsions, etc., and permits school administrators to potentially prevent the enrollment of students who may be harmful to themselves or others.

Preparatory Steps or Programs to Intercept Potential Violent Incidents in Schools

Chapter 3

Our Very Smart, Violent Children

Introductory Comments

One of the foremost responsibilities of school administrators is to adopt preparatory programs or "steps" that are designed to intercept or prevent a potential violent incident in schools.

Designed to protect students and school employees, the outlined programs in Chapter Three (3) are intended to achieve this goal; the deployment of school resource officers, a school "silent observer" program, threat management procedures and training, and a general school security plan are the most essential elements or preparatory steps that should be adopted by a school district.

Additionally, there were programs outlined in Chapter Two (2) that will assist the school administrator during this effort, i.e., School Disciplinary Procedures – Rules of Conduct, etc. The development of an efficient information retrieval and management system about "student conduct" is, for example, a very important part of this responsibility.

And, finally, it is essential that schools develop a strong "partnership" with law enforcement, the office of the prosecuting attorney, the courts, and other service providers in the community, i.e., mental health, etc. There is a mutual need to work together and jointly attempt to prevent or respond to any potential or actual criminal activity in the school environment.

School Resource Officer Program

Brief Summary

Programs regarding school-police partnerships should be adopted or expanded. In particular, it is recommended that school districts assign police officers to at least high school facilities or, at their discretion, other school buildings.

Directly accountable to the school superintendents or assigned school principals, School Resource Officers will assist schools, communities, and local police departments in many very important ways: prevent and control violent activity, perform general security duties for schools, become part of other vital school programs, i.e., student counseling, tutoring and mentoring, liaison with local law enforcement, etc. Very importantly, School Resource Officers would become the "first responders" to any critical incident or serious problems in their assigned school.

School "Silent Observer" Program

Brief Summary

Schools should adopt a student "silent observer" program that encourages students to confidentially report activity or behavior in the schools or community that appears, at the very least, to endanger others. This program, combined with a relatively small reward system, successfully exists in districts around the country.

Additionally, all school employees should accept the responsibility of "information retrieval" and confidentially report suspected activity to a centralized source in the school, or district, for proper disposition. It should be remembered that the most important tool to prevent violent activity in schools or communities is the retrieval, assessment, and response to information or "intelligence" about potential problems or criminal activity.

Threat Management Program

Brief Summary

One of the most difficult responsibilities of school administrators and employees is responding to a "threat" – threats to detonate "bombs," kill school employees and students, or other forms of lethal activity that potentially affects many lives in a school facility. It is a very arduous task that appears to be increasingly occurring in schools around the country.

Because of this reason, school administrators are frequently searching for answers to questions about how to respond to such threats and are very needful for a procedure, together with a training program, that will assist them and their employees. School employees want to know, for example, about the proper initial response to a threat, the roles of law enforcement and other emergency service providers, the responsibilities of school employees directly after a threat is discovered or conveyed, how to retrieve and manage information or "intelligence" about potential suspects, and how to control or manage rumors. School administrators need to know how they should work with their school board, school employees, parents, and the community after a threat is received and the initial response is completed. Many questions about general "school security" and the safety of students and employees are or will be asked by a variety of fearful sources, and the administrators want to respond assuredly and correctly.

Also, there are many questions regarding the disposition, i.e., suspension, expulsion, arrest, and adjudication procedures, etc., of the identified or apprehended suspects, criminally and internally. And, finally, there are many viewpoints among school administrators about securing school facilities and "control" of student activities after a threat is received.

The answers to all of these critical questions

must become comprehensively outlined in a procedure that is individually adopted by all of our schools – it should reflect the policies of the local school board and administrators and respond to the needs of their district. Because of this reason, a single, uniform procedure for all school districts may not conform to local policies or practices and is not a practical method of achieving this goal. Furthermore, the process of developing a local or "customized" procedure about "Threat Management" should include local law enforcement and the office of the prosecuting attorney; their opinions about legal and enforcement matters are a vital resource for school administrators during this effort.

After the procedure is developed, a training program should be designed and presented to all school employees – knowledge about the procedure will encourage employees to respond to a "threat" in a more unified, coordinated, and efficient manner.

Our Very Smart, Violent Children

General School Building Security Plans

Brief Summary

General school building security plans, procedures, and technology are absolutely essential and, after professional consultation, should be adopted or installed to control building access, monitor activity, and protect school property. However, it must be remembered that this kind of equipment and related procedures, for the most part, are not designed to prevent violent critical incidents in school facilities and should be "customized" for each school facility pursuant to identified needs.

Responses to Violent Incidents in Schools

Chapter 4

Introductory Comments

The most graphic way to begin this Chapter is to briefly repeat and extend the hypothetical "incident" that is outlined in the Foreword:

"It was the beginning of another day at the high school. The students were in the hallways, gathered around their lockers, or in the large cafeteria, enjoying their friendships or quietly preparing for the day. The mood was good – friendly and peaceful. After all, it was a 'good' school – academically and socially.

"Until the awful sound of gunfire erupted.

"At first, some believed it was simply fireworks being playfully discharged. But these thoughts were quickly erased by the dreadful sights and sounds of students screaming, running, and falling to the floor, covered with blood from wounds to their heads and young bodies.

"Some were dead, others were seriously injured and desperately crying for help. And the gunfire persisted, striking more students and some of the teachers.

"Near the middle of the hysterical crowd, another student stood – with a gun in his hand. Without speaking, he calmly aimed and fired his weapon, frequently reloading and deliberately firing again. And again.

"Everyone knew him. He was a very 'smart' student, possessed a high grade point average, and loved computers. He appeared alone a lot but was never in trouble at school.

"And there he was – trying to kill everyone.

"Why was he doing this?"

At the moment, nobody was thinking about calling 9-1-1 or the police; survival – getting away from that lethal gun – was the only thought in the minds of everyone. Lying breathlessly on the floor, beneath a table or desk, going to a restroom – anywhere that would safely conceal or protect them.

Eventually, the sounds of the gunfire stopped, and someone near a telephone called 9-1-1 – about ten (10) minutes after it all began.

Inexplicably, the young man with the gun suddenly went to another part of the building. A few minutes later, the sound of the weapon was heard again. One shot – and, for a moment, it became very quiet. Except for the sounds from the wounded students and teachers – they were still crying and asking for help. A few teachers, disregarding their own personal safety, desperately tried to help – trying to stop the bleeding or simply consoling them. Other students ran to the exits of the building, not knowing if the suspect or an incendiary device was waiting for them near a doorway or in one of the adjacent hallways.

A few minutes after the 9-1-1 call was received, the first police units began to arrive at the school building; they immediately requested "tactical" and bomb disposal teams to respond and assist them.

Simultaneously, television and radio news crews, after monitoring the police radio frequencies, arrived at the school and began to remotely broadcast "live" reports about the incident and interview hysterical students who had fled from the building.

And, eventually, hundreds of distraught parents, family members, and friends of the students and school employees came to the school – searching for someone to ask about the welfare of their children or their loved ones.

Countless other people, after becoming informed about the incident, attempted to go to the school – causing the general access to the building to become completely congested or "grid-locked."

Initially, there was no communication between the entrapped occupants in the school and the police or anyone outside of the facility – no one was answering the telephone calls to the school, and no one was calling anyone from it. No information – about the injured or the suspect.

The police secured the "outer perimeter" of the school, attempted to identify and interview witnesses, and quickly organized a plan to tactically enter the facility; emergency medical technicians arrived at the scene and began to coordinate their activities with the police.

Outside of the school, district administrators and others were being asked questions about the number and identities of the deceased or injured students and employees, the identity of the suspect, and the reasons for committing the deadly assault – questions that were, at the moment, unanswerable.

And, during the next several minutes, everything appeared to become worse – still no word from or about the occupants in the school, and the environment outside of the building was becoming increasingly congested, frustrating, and stressful.

This is a very brief portrayal of the first twenty (20) minutes of a violent incident – all of these events could occur directly after the first shot is fired in a school building; it is the most critical time period – for the affected students, school employees, and all of the people responsible for their safety.

One of the reasons for attempting to realistically outline this "incident" and the responses to it was to develop a virtual sense of awareness – and to encourage our schools to become more prepared for this kind of potential tragedy, intellectually and emotionally.

And it could occur – in any school or community. At any time.

There are many lessons for everyone – law enforcement, journalists, emergency service providers, parents, etc.

But, at the moment, the most important message is for our school administrators, teachers, support employees, and students. It is about their personal safety and responsibilities – their very important duties that are intended to protect lives during those first critical minutes after a shooting begins in a school facility – and temporarily performing those tasks without police or emergency medical services next to them in a very hysterical, deadly environment.

And that is the goal of this Chapter and the Appendix – to strongly encourage our schools and public safety services to jointly adopt procedures and training programs about responses to violent incidents in schools and to outline a Model General Procedure for Schools about How to Respond to Violent Incidents in Schools.

The Need for Procedures and Training Programs

Brief Summary

Detailed procedures and related training programs for school, police, emergency medical, and fire services personnel regarding the responses to and the management of violent incidents in schools must be prepared and adopted.

All school buildings should possess a procedure that outlines the role and responsibilities of all school employees (see Appendix: How to Respond to Violent Incidents: A General Procedure for Schools); this document should also outline, for example, communication procedures, guidelines about personal safety, liaison duties with law enforcement, etc.

All police departments should possess a

procedure that clearly specifies the responsibilities of all police employees during the management of the critical incident response; this document should also list, for example, the duties of tactical and other specialized units, investigatory and forensic assignments, communication procedures, the roles of "mutual aid" respondents, etc.

The planning process of this effort must be jointly conducted to ensure maximum coordination and response efficiency; a single, general procedure for each school district and public safety personnel may become the result of this combined effort. Additionally, a combined training program, consisting of at least school administrators and public safety managers or command staff, should be initially and annually conducted in a manner that combines classroom material with a "simulated incident" training exercise and "response critique briefing."

Crisis Management Team Program

Brief Summary

The role and responsibilities of Crisis Management Teams in our school districts should be supported. Post-incident victim or witness counseling services or general assistance is a vital part of any critical incident Response Management Plan and must be coordinated with the law enforcement-school response procedures.

The Process of Developing Community and Financial Support for Programs

Conclusion

The Process of Developing Community and Financial Support for Programs

To strongly encourage the adoption of very important programs or a "model plan" that is designed to respond to a growing problem that is affecting or afflicting many children always appears unfinished unless there are at least some recommendations about how to develop support for them in our schools and communities.

And that is the intent of these final paragraphs: to insert a few thoughts about this process and the need to build a community coalition that shares the vision and commitment to the goals of this book.

It all begins with community meetings; school board members, school administrators, teachers and support staff, elected officials and administrators from the local governmental unit, law enforcement administrators and staff, community service providers (i.e., mental health, health, drug and alcohol prevention or treatment programs, etc.), service groups (i.e., Rotary International, etc.), Chamber of Commerce or community business leadership, volunteer groups (i.e., Big Brothers and Sisters, etc.), and, most importantly, the students and parents of the community should be invited.

Facilitated by a respected community member, the agenda of the very participatory meetings would consist of:

1. a brief outline of the identified needs or problems affecting children;

2. the need to adopt a clear community vision or goals; and

3. a summary of the recommended programs that directly respond to the identified needs or problems.

The general intent of the meetings is to "hear the people" about the aforementioned issues and eventually develop a consensual statement from the community that identifies needs or problems, their "vision" or goals, and a plan or programs that they feel are vitally necessary in their community.

At this point, or directly after the community meetings, administrators from the schools, law enforcement, the local governmental unit, community services, and other identified organizations should meet and begin the process of collaboratively planning, organizing, staffing, managing, and financially supporting the programs that were identified by the community. This joint developmental effort will become, at a very early stage, a discussion about the availability of fiscal resources, i.e., program staffing, operating costs, and other related expenses.

One of the reasons for recommending this planning or program development process is to discourage the assignment of all program costs to a single organization – the schools. If that occurred, the "affordability" of a program becomes less and it competes, for example, with other essential curriculum appropriations. It is necessary, therefore, to develop a more expanded fiscal plan that not only increases potential financial resources but also reflects, again, the intent of bringing together the entire community. All of the service providers share very important program development responsibilities including planning, organizing, budgeting, and managing.

With a very clear view of the "community vision," the administrators should:

1. outline a general "blueprint" or operating plan – i.e., the type and amount of services to be rendered, minimum staffing plan, approximated operating costs, etc. – for each of the identified programs that are intended to become adopted;

2. review their individual operating budgets for the current fiscal year and attempt to identify existing financial resources or employee positions that may be assigned to the proposed program operating plans, i.e., police officers or deputy sheriffs assigned to tutorial or mentoring programs, youth workers coordinating recreational, social, and community service programs, etc.;

3. approach local units of government – commissions, councils, and boards consisting of elected officials – and request financial support to supplement identified appropriations in their own operating budgets that may be assigned to the programs;

4. seek grant awards from federal and state authorities and private foundations that may support any program activities (only after steps two (2) and three (3) are completed); and

5. meet with community businesses and service groups with the intent of developing partnerships or other sources of financial and volunteer support that may complement the aforementioned efforts and encourage program participation.

There are many other options regarding the development of financial support for the outlined programs, but the most essential, general steps are listed. Because of a very critical need for this kind of programming in our schools and communities, the financial development process is extremely important and an essential part of any planning process.

Finally, a personal thought about this issue: the author strongly believes that a millage request, partly designed to support the outlined programs, is absolutely necessary and probably very "supportable" by communities. But, admittedly, this opinion is being expressed without any political acuity or skills. After all, what does an old, battered police chief know about political matters?

How to Respond to Violent Incidents:
A General Procedure for Schools

Appendix

How to Respond to Violent Incidents:
A General Procedure for Schools

William G. Hegarty
Chief of Police, ret.

Robert Goethal
Police Captain, ret.
Director of Security
Rockford Public Schools

Larry Johnson
Former Police Sergeant
Director of Public Safety
Grand Rapids Public Schools

With Steven W. Dieleman

How to Respond to Violent Incidents: A General Procedure for Schools

A. Purpose

The general purpose of this Procedure is to outline the responsibilities of school employees and students during responses to violent critical incidents in schools.

B. Goals

The goals of this Procedure are to:

1. prevent the loss of life and serious injury to students and school employees;

2. safely control the activity of suspects until relieved by police units; and

3. conduct the response to violent critical incidents in schools in a coordinated,

efficient, and safe manner.

C. General Procedure

The outline of this Procedure is intended to chronologically list the general responsibilities of all school employees and students during responses to violent critical incidents in schools.

A critical incident is any person, in or adjacent to a school facility, displaying or discharging a weapon and potentially or actually causing loss of life or serious personal injury.

Beginning with the initial report of the aforementioned incident, this Procedure attempts to outline the general responses and duties for school employees and students. It should be remembered that a "critical incident" may unexpectedly become a hostage or armed, barricaded person situation or an incident with detonated incendiary devices; because of this reason, this Procedure contingently outlines the responsibilities that school administrators may wish to adopt for their employees and students.

D. Initial Responsibilities

If any person – student, school employee, or visitor – observes any person with a firearm in or adjacent to a school facility or event, it must be reported immediately to the central office of the facility or a designated authority. If the threat to the personal safety of any person is imminent, the steps outlined in this Procedure shall be promptly completed.

After receiving a report of a critical incident or an armed person in or adjacent to a school facility, the central office will:

1. if necessary, attempt to verify it;

2. immediately broadcast "Code Red" to all employees and students, together with a codified general location of the threat; this broadcast should recur every ten (10) seconds for at least one (1) minute (see Section L – Definitions, "Code Red Broadcast," etc.);

3. promptly call 9-1-1 or notify emergency personnel about the nature of the threat and state the location, identity or description of

the suspect, the type and amount of weapons possessed by the suspect, information about injuries, etc.;

4. document the date and time of the Code Red broadcasts and the 9-1-1 emergency call; and

5. notify the office of the Superintendent of the incident.

Furthermore, it is extremely important to promptly control access to the school facility or any part of a school facility that is potentially or actually affected by the threat or assault. The initial control or containment of suspect activity is absolutely critical: for example, securely closing fire doors or other physical "barricades" directly after the threat or assault is reported may help achieve this goal and, if properly completed, not cause unnecessary risk to students or employees. Finally, if a school resource officer, i.e., police officer, is employed by or assigned to the school facility, he or she should be contacted immediately and directed to promptly respond to the location of the threat with the intent of apprehending the suspect.

E. Responsibilities of Teachers

The general responsibilities of teachers:

1. Promptly and safely go to or stay in their assigned classroom and attempt to direct students and employees in the adjacent hallway to their classroom.

2. If any student or employee is injured, attempt to assist them to their classroom for emergency medical care and safety.

3. If the Code Red broadcast does not imminently affect them or their classroom, and their room is adjacent to or near fire doors, they should promptly and safely close and "wedge" the doors for the purpose of prohibiting access to their hallway and all of the occupied classrooms.

4. After the hallway is "cleared" of students and employees, enter their room, lock or secure the door, turn the room lights off and, if possible, conceal windows, i.e., close blinds, shades, etc.

5. Direct the room occupants to assist them by

placing desks, tables, chairs, etc., against the least observable wall and direct all room occupants to lie in the space between the wall and the furniture, i.e., arranged to provide maximum concealment and security.

6. Direct all of the room occupants to remain calm and quiet at all times.

7. Count the number of occupants in a room and, if safely permitted, attempt to identify them.

8. Telephonically report to the central office their room number, name, and the number of occupants in the room, together with any unusual needs, i.e., emergency medical or personal health problems, etc.

9. Attempt to administer emergency treatment to room occupants in a concealed and safe manner.

10. Do not permit anyone to leave the room for any reason until they are directed or "cleared" by the central office or the police.

11. Attempt to safely observe and report to the central office any information that may be

related to the activity of a suspect in the proximity of their rooms, i.e., statements by the suspect, physical descriptors or the identity of the suspect, the sound of weapons being discharged, etc.

12. DO NOT ATTEMPT TO CONFRONT OR APPREHEND A SUSPECT AT ANY TIME.

13. If they are unavoidably confronted by a suspect, do not display disagreement, anger, hostility, or any behavior that may precipitate a violent response.

14. Stay in their room until they are directed to leave or "evacuate" it by the central office or police. They will be requested to leave the room after it is:

   a. reasonably determined that it is relatively safe, i.e., clear of any suspect activity or incendiary devices, i.e., bombs, or;

   b. determined that the activity of the suspect is "controlled" and there is no reason to believe that evacuation is harmful to the room occupants.

15. After they are directed to leave the room, they will be advised of the route of departure, the proper building exit, and the designated assembly point away from the school facility.

16. They should remove any record or document regarding student attendance from their room and eventually present it to a designated school employee responsible for the accountability of all school students and employees.

17. At the designated assembly point, all evacuated students and school employees shall:

    a. not provide statements to or comply with requests from news organizations, i.e., news media; and

    b. await transportation to a secured site for further disposition.

F. Responsibilities of Other School Employees

The responsibilities of other school employees,

i.e., athletic department staff, food service employees, library, and custodial staff, etc.:

1. Promptly and safely respond to or stay in school facilities of larger assemblies of students, i.e., cafeteria, library, auditorium, gymnasium, etc.

2. Comply with the general procedures that are outlined in the "Responsibilities of Teachers" section.

3. If the physical properties of the room do not permit completion of the aforementioned procedure, i.e., there may be fixed, collapsible seating in an auditorium, etc., direct the room occupants to positions of the most practical concealment and security, i.e., lie on the floor against the walls in the gymnasium or, if collapsible seating permits in an auditorium, direct all room occupants to sit on the floor directly in front of the raised seat and to lower their heads and upper bodies to a point that is directly above their thighs and knees, etc.

4. School employees assigned to these responsibilities should be equipped with portable radios and maintain communication with the central office or "internal command post."

5. They should report to the central office their location, the approximate number of persons in their room or facility, any emergency or unusual needs, i.e., medical or personal health problems, etc., and any information about suspect activity.

6. If it is safe and practical, administer necessary emergency medical assistance to room occupants in a concealed and safe manner.

7. DO NOT ATTEMPT TO CONFRONT OR APPREHEND A SUSPECT AT ANY TIME.

8. If unavoidably confronted by a suspect, do not display disagreement, anger, hostility, or any behavior that may precipitate a violent response.

9. Stay in the room until directed to leave or

"evacuate" it by the central office or police. Employees and students will be requested to leave the room after it is:

a. reasonably determined that it is relatively safe, i.e., clear of any suspect activity or incendiary devices, i.e., bombs; or

b. determined that the activity of the suspect is "controlled" and there is no reason to believe that evacuation is harmful to the room occupants.

10. After they are directed to leave the room, employees will be advised of the route of departure, the proper building exit, and the designated assembly point away from the school facility.

11. It is very important that all room occupants completely and promptly comply with the aforementioned rules.

12. At the designated assembly point, all evacuated students and school employees shall:

a. not provide statements or comply with requests from news organizations, i.e., news media; and

b. await transportation to a secured site for further disposition.

G. Responsibilities of the School Response Team

The responsibilities of the School Response Team are critical; they are responsible for the control of suspect activity and are deployed to prevent loss of life and serious personal injury to any student or school employee.

The School Response Team shall consist of an assistant principal or supervisor, School Resource Officer or security staff, school counselor, custodial employee, and any other employee who can assist the Team during these very critical assignments.

Equipped with portable radios, the School Response Team shall respond to a designated assembly point identified by the supervisor directly after a Code Red broadcast is rendered. At the assembly point, the Team Supervisor will receive from the central office or "internal command post" any further detailed information about suspect activity and attempt to organize, with the assistance of the Team, a "plan of response." After this plan is formulated, the Team will:

1. promptly and safely proceed to the proximity of the potential or actual assault;

2. direct students and employees to rooms or positions of safety;

3. attempt to contain or "barricade" the suspect or physically prohibit the suspect access to any other parts of the building; and

4. with the help of a counselor, attempt to safely communicate with the suspect after building access is controlled.

A School Response Team will NOT attempt to confront and apprehend an armed suspect; however, the School Resource Officer, assigned to the Team and pursuant to the authority of his position and the rules of his department, may exert any "level of force" that is necessary to prevent the loss of life or serious injury to any person.

Again, the foremost responsibility of the Team is

to control the activity of the suspect in a prompt and safe manner. Accordingly, the physical resources of the building, i.e., fire doors, etc., may be the most important "tools" to achieve these goals.

The Team members should possess, together with their two-channel portable radios, any other equipment that will protect them.

All Team members should attend both initial and annual training workshops that outline a variety of subjects related to their duties, i.e., tactical procedures for School Response Teams, radio communication procedures, identification of incendiary devices, working with local law enforcement, etc.

H. Responsibilities of Administrators – Central Office or Internal Command Post

After receiving a report of a critical incident or of an armed person in or adjacent to a school facility, the central office or internal command post will complete the "Initial Responsibilities" that are outlined in Section D of this Procedure.

Additionally, central office employees will:

1. Verify the deployment of the School Response Team and eventually convey all of the identified details of the incident to the supervisor of the Team, i.e., the same information that is conveyed to the 9-1-1 operator.

2. Immediately assign employees to the responsibilities of:

   a. internal telephone communications — Assigned employees shall receive internal telephone messages, i.e., from classrooms or other school rooms, coordinate and respond to requests for assistance, etc. Internal telephone messages about suspect activity are extremely important and shall be promptly conveyed to the police, the supervisor of the School Response Team, and school employees who may be affected.

   b. portable radio communications — Assigned employees shall receive portable radio messages from the School Response Team and other assigned school employees; record, coordinate, or respond to radio communication requests. Because of the duties of the School Response Team, this is a critical responsibility, and those assigned to it must work directly with other school employees and the police to ensure the proper coordination and dissemination of information. Additionally, the responsibility of viewing internal video monitors and communicating directly with the School Response Team about observed activity is part of this assignment.

c. student and employee accountability – This responsibility is critical, and those assigned to it must work directly with the internal telephone and portable radio communications assignments; the sources of information about the identity, location, and physical condition of all students and employees can only be assessed, for the most part, by telephone and radio communications, and the responsibility for developing this "personal inventory" can be most efficiently accomplished in this centralized manner.

d. liaison with the external command post – The purpose of this very important assignment is to provide an informational "bridge" between the secured school facility and other authorities or vital services that are located outside the affected building, i.e., office of the Superintendent, law enforcement, emergency medical services, bomb disposal and canine teams, "parent liaison services," public information, etc. This assignment will receive, coordinate, or convey information that will facilitate the response to the incident by the police and other service providers.

The proper staffing of these responsibilities is critical. A school district may wish to adopt a "school mutual aid" procedure that directs selected employees from other school facilities to respond to any school facility that is affected by a critical incident or other emergency situation for the purpose of promptly and properly staffing the outlined assignments.

I. Responsibilities of Support Services – External Command Post

The external command post, located adjacent to or near the affected school facility, shall consist of the listed authorities and services:

1. Office of the Superintendent – for matters regarding final district authority and the dissemination of all public information;

2. Legal services – for consultation regarding district, school, or employee liability;

3. Transportation – to promptly receive and deploy, if necessary, transportation vehicles, i.e., busses, vans, etc.;

4. Building and grounds – for assistance about matters related to building HVAC systems, floor plans, etc.;

5. Financial management for business – for emergency authorization to purchase urgent goods and services;

6. Parent-family services – to provide information or services to the affected parents and families of students, employees, etc.;

7. Communications – to monitor, receive, and transmit messages to the school internal communications or central office personnel and to facilitate communication with police and other responding emergency services;

8. Event recorder – to chronologically record, in summary form, the major events, assignments, decisions, and other directed matters regarding incident responses and descriptively "plot," in the context of a school floor plan, the locations of students and employees;

9. District/school counselors, social workers –

to counsel authorities about the personal history and "psychological profile" of identified suspects, together with other related matters, i.e., identity of family members, friends, etc.;

10. Crisis management team leader – to become informed about the nature of the incident for the purpose of providing grief counseling services after police "clearance" is rendered;

11. Public safety services – the command post and communications center for all police, emergency medical, fire services, utility services, etc.

It is vitally necessary for all of the aforementioned authorities and services to work closely together and support, in a very coordinated manner, the police response to critical incidents in school facilities.

J. Responsibilities of Students

1. Promptly and calmly go to the nearest

attended room or assigned classroom; do not loiter, look for friends, go to the restroom, or engage in any other activity.

2. Obey the teachers or school employees at all times.

3. Place desks, tables, chairs, etc., against the least observable wall in a secured, attended classroom or room and lie in the space between the furniture and the wall. Stay concealed at all times.

4. Do not attempt to talk to or apprehend a suspect at any time.

5. If you are unavoidably confronted by a suspect, do not display disagreement, anger, hostility, or any behavior that may cause a violent response. Act compliantly.

6. Do not leave secured rooms for any reason until you are directed by the proper authority.

K. Personal Safety Responsibilities

If any person is unprotected and unable to go to

an attended, secured room, or comply with the content of this Procedure and has, at least, visual contact with a suspect, he or she should:

1. attempt to find physical concealment as soon as possible; if this cannot be achieved, lie against a wall or any other physical structure that may provide at least partial body security;

2. not display disagreement, anger, hostility, or any behavior that may cause a violent response;

3. leave the area directly after the level of risk becomes minimized and promptly seek the nearest assistance or attended, secured room.

L. Definitions

Internal Command Post – The internal command post is any secured office or room in a school facility that is affected by a critical incident. It may be the office of the principal or central office, the office of an assistant principal or security office, or a designated room that is safely distant from the threat or assault and in the proximity of a building access point.

External Command Post – The external command post is any secured location adjacent to or near the affected school facility that will provide centralized support services during and directly after the response to a critical incident.

Code Red Broadcast – This is the codified notification or broadcast that alerts all students and employees of a potential or actual violent criminal incident in a school facility. The term "Code Red" designates the type of incident. Additionally, the Code Red broadcast should include a code that identifies the general location, building section, or "wing" of the incident, together with the number of the floor. For example, all school building sections should be pre-designated with an "alpha" symbol, i.e., Adam, Baker, Charlie, etc., or North, South, East, or West. Building floor numbers are identified numerically. If the incident were occurring on the first floor of the "A" wing of a building, the broadcast would be "Code Red – Adam One." If the incident were occurring on the second floor of the West wing of a building, the broadcast would be "Code Red – West Two." The intent of this codified designation is to prevent employees and students from unknowingly entering a part of a school facility that is dangerously affected by a critical incident. The incident alert should be broadcast every ten (10) seconds for at least one (1) minute directly after the incident is reported.